LAND OF THE FREE

The White House

Anne Hempstead

Heinemann Library
Chicago, Illinois

© 2006 Heinemann
Published by Heinemann Library
A division of Reed Elsevier Inc.
Chicago, IL
Customer Service 888-363-4266
Visit our website at www.heinemannraintree.com

For more information address the publisher:
Raintree, 100 N. LaSalle, Suite 1200, Chicago IL 60602

Printed in China by WKT Company Limited

10 09 08 07 06
10 9 8 7 6 5 4 3 2 1

ISBN 1-4034-6999-7 (hc) -- ISBN 1-4034-7006-5 (pb)

Library of Congress Cataloging-in-Publication Data:
Cataloging-in-publication data is on file at the Library of Congress.

Photo research by Julie Laffin

Acknowledgments
The author and publisher are grateful to the following for permission to reproduce copyright material:
p.4 © Peter Gridley/Getty Images, p.6 © Corbis/ Swim Ink 2, LLC,
p.7a, 7c © Getty Images/PhotoDisc, p.7b © Corbis, p.8 Smithsonian Institution,
p.11 © Corbis/Marco Cristofori, p. 13 The Granger Collection, p.15 © Corbis/Bettmann,
pp.16, 18, 21, 24 © AP/Wide World Photos, p.22 Jimmy Carter Library,
p.27 © Corbis/Zefa/Larry Dale Gordon.

Cover photo: © Getty Images/Taxi/Walter Bibikow

The paper used to print this book comes from sustainable resources.

Contents

Chapter One:
1600 Pennsylvania Avenue

The White House is the official home and workplace of the president of the United States. For over 200 years, every president since John Adams has lived in the White House. Within its walls, U.S. presidents make serious decisions concerning the nation and the world. In its historic rooms, presidents and their families live and play. The White House is also a museum. Over the years it has become a treasure house of beautiful and historic objects.

The White House is a place where America shows its pride and **patriotism**. The White House is known as "The People's House," because the White House belongs to the people of the United States. It is the only home of a world leader that is open regularly to people, free of charge. Americans are invited to the White House to celebrate national holidays, to honor heroes, to welcome leaders from around the world, or to tour the grounds. In the spirit of **democracy**, Americans also gather outside the White House to show approval for the president or protest against government policies.

Symbol of the presidency

The United States has many **symbols**. The flag, the bald eagle, and the Statue of Liberty are just some of the symbols that have **patriotic** meanings. Over time, the White House has come to be known around the world as the symbol of the U.S. presidency. For many people, when they look at a picture of the White House, they think not only of the building but also of the idea of leadership. Often the term "White House" is used to mean the president. For example, when a newspaper reports that the White House announced a new education program, it means that the president and his administration have announced a new program.

Washington, D.C.: home to the White House

The White House is located in Washington, D.C., the nation's capital. Washington serves as the center or seat for the **federal** government. All three branches of the government are based in Washington. The Congress, part of the **legislative branch**, meets at the Capitol Building. The Supreme Court, part of the **judicial branch**, hears cases in the Supreme Court Building. The president, who is the head of the **executive branch**, lives and works at the White House.

I WANT YOU
FOR U.S. ARMY
NEAREST RECRUITING STATION

Uncle Sam has been a popular symbol of the United States since World War I.

A system of checks and balances

The United States government has three branches. The three branches provide for a system of checks and balances. This means that no one branch will have too much power over the other two.

President's power
- *Enforces laws*
- ***Vetoes***, *or overrules, bills from Congress*
- *Writes budget for the running of the government*
- *Appoints judges*
- *Makes agreements with other countries— with the approval of Congress*

Congress's power
- *Makes laws*
- *Votes on taxes*
- *Approves judges appointed by the president*
- *Has the power to remove the president or justices from office for misconduct*

Supreme Court's power
- *Makes sure the laws passed by Congress are constitutional*
- *Decides if actions taken by the president follow the Constitution*

Chapter Two:
A Presidential Palace

After the Revolutionary War, the new nation was faced with many challenges. Since 1784 the government had moved from city to city thirteen times. If the new nation was to be stable and lasting, the government needed a permanent **capital** city.

In 1790 Congress voted for a capital city to be established along the Potomac River between Virginia and Maryland. President George Washington was given the job of overseeing the planning and building of the new city. To help him, Washington hired a brilliant French artist and engineer, Pierre-Charles L'Enfant.

L'Enfant made a plan for a "democratic" city that would rival, but not copy, the great capitals of Europe. The plan called for broad avenues and magnificent buildings. Buildings would be open to the public and citizens would be able to mingle and talk with members of Congress and the president. To show the separate but equal powers of the government, L'Enfant placed the "Meeting House" for Congress and the "President's Palace" at opposite ends of a wide connecting boulevard–what would later be known as Pennsylvania Avenue. L'Enfant's plan was new and original, just like the United States itself.

The contest

In 1792 a contest was announced for a design for the President's House. George Washington understood how important the president's house would be for the nation. He wanted a building that would reflect a strong and stable government, so he insisted that it be built of stone. He suggested that presidents should live and work at the presidential mansion. It was his vision for a grand and elegant building that would become an enduring **symbol** of the leadership of the president.

James Hoban, an Irish **architect** and builder, won the contest and the $500 prize. Hoban based his design on the palace of the Duke of Leinster in Dublin, Ireland. His plan called for an elegant three-story stone structure with columns and an eagle carved above the front door.

The classical Greek and Roman details of Hoban's design were considered very appropriate for a presidential mansion. The country's Constitution was based on the ideals of the ancient civilizations of Greece and Rome. Now the country's buildings were also being based on the ideals of those civilizations.

Thomas Jefferson, an amateur architect himself, liked the idea of developing an American style. He believed that architecture based on Greek and Roman styles would inspire **patriotism**. Classical buildings became a way to display through bricks and mortar the democratic ideals of those ancient societies. Domes, temple fronts, columns, and other Greek and Roman details began to be used in the design of homes, churches, and public buildings. Hoban's design was exactly what George Washington was looking for in a home for the nation's president.

On October 13, 1792, construction began on the mansion. When it was finished over eight years later, it was as grand yet simple as Washington had wished. The president's home was as elegant as a palace but as comfortable as a country house. Sadly, George Washington never spent one night in the President's House. He died before it was completed.

Roman ruins such as these had a large influence on early American architects.

The president moves in

When President John Adams moved to Washington in 1800, the house was not quite finished. But before the plaster had dried, the President's House opened it doors to the public to become "The People's House."

Hoban had designed the White House to have three floors. Each floor was to have its own use. The ground floor was for the kitchen, laundry, and heating equipment. The second, the "public floor," had large rooms with high ceilings and a grand entrance. This floor was where the president would live, work, and meet and entertain visitors. The third floor was an attic.

It was always difficult to keep the public and private uses of the mansion separated. Abigail Adams invited guests to the private family rooms because the public rooms were not finished. She also had to hang the family's laundry to dry in the East Room. There was no fence surrounding the yard, and she did not think the public should see the president's dirty laundry. During the Civil War, Union troops slept in the East Room. Since then, the room has been used as a performance hall, a site for weddings, and a location for signing important legislation.

The smoky house

According to a famous story, the president's house is known as the White House because it was painted white to hide the scorch marks from the 1814 fire. The truth is that the building was originally referred to as the Presidential Palace or Presidential Mansion. Dolley Madison called it the "Presidential Castle." About three years before the fire, people started referring to it as the White House because of its whitewashed exterior. In 1901 President Theodore Roosevelt made the name official.

Residents of D.C. flee the 1814 fire.

Fire

In 1809 James Madison and his wife Dolley came to live in the White House. Dolley was known for her skills as a hostess. Congressmen and diplomats flocked to the president's home to enjoy the comfortable social atmosphere.

As the White House neared completion, disaster struck. In 1814, during the War of 1812, invading British troops set the house on fire. The flames destroyed the inside of the mansion. Knowing enemy troops were coming, Dolley Madison fled the house, taking a portrait of George Washington and some silver with her for safe keeping. The Madisons returned to find only the White House walls still standing. It was important to show the world that the United States had endured, however, so the president's house needed to be rebuilt immediately. On New Year's Day, 1818, President James Monroe held an open house reception—wet paint, wet plaster, and all.

The people's house

During the 1800s, the White House became a **symbol** of American **democracy**, just as George Washington had hoped it would. Thomas Jefferson thought that the house was too grand for the leader of a **democracy**. But when he became president in 1801 he made it even bigger. He built terraced **pavilions** on the sides for stables and storage. Following his strong ideas of democracy, Jefferson opened the house to the public each morning. He enjoyed greeting visitors in his riding clothes or his dressing gown.

Sometimes people have not behaved very well in "The People's House." One such occasion was the **inauguration** of Andrew Jackson. After watching Jackson take the oath of office on Capitol Hill, a mob of people marched to the White House looking for food and drink. The unruly crowd stood on the furniture with their muddy boots and broke thousands of dollars worth of china and crystal trying to get to the refreshments. Jackson escaped from the chaos and spent the night in a nearby hotel.

In the 1820s, two porticoes—porches whose roofs are supported with columns—were built. With these additions, the exterior of the White House took the form that we know today. In 1947 President Truman realized that the White House had become a beloved symbol when he spent $10,000 to add a second-floor balcony. Many people objected to the change, claiming that it destroyed the familiar look of the White House. Truman was able to keep the balcony, but the U.S. twenty-dollar bill, which carried the image of the White House, had to be redesigned and reprinted. Eventually everyone accepted the new image of the People's House.

In 1901, when President Theodore Roosevelt moved into the White House with his wife and six children, they discovered that it was too crowded. The offices of the president and his staff were on the second floor along with the family's bedrooms. Congress gave $65,000 for the construction of an office area west of the White House and a new entrance wing to the east. On November 6, 1902, Roosevelt held the first meeting in the new Cabinet Room of the West Wing.

President Harry Truman declares victory in World War II from his desk in the Oval Office.

Chapter Three:
Working in the White House

The White House has been called the president's "workshop of **democracy**." It is the center from which he performs his job as the nation's head-of-state. One of his duties is to be the United States's main **diplomat**. He works with world leaders to discuss issues and solve problems that arise between countries. The president travels worldwide as a representative of the United States. While in the United States, he welcomes many important people to the White House for receptions, conferences, and meetings.

Ambassadors and other distinguished guests usually begin their visit to the White House in the Diplomatic Reception Room. During World War II, President Franklin Roosevelt made radio broadcasts to the country from the Diplomatic Reception Room and turned the room next door, the Map Room, into his war room. Maps showing the progress of the war helped the president decide on military strategy.

Important staterooms

Guests often have dinner in the State Dining Room. Today it seats 140 people, but originally it was much smaller. Thomas Jefferson used a part of it for his office. In 1902 the room was remodeled to create a large dining room, which President Theodore Roosevelt decorated with hunting trophies and a stuffed moose head.

Some of the staterooms are named for the color of their decorations. The Blue Room, one of three oval shaped rooms in the White House, is used as a small reception room. It was the first and only room in which a president, Grover Cleveland, was married. The Green Room was originally designed as a dining room. It is believed that Thomas Jefferson chose the color for it.

Dolley Madison hosted small, fashionable parties in the Red Room. It has since been used as a music room and

First Lady Nancy Reagan was fond of the Red Room.

Lincoln's bedroom

The Lincoln Bedroom is now a famous guest room in the White House—but it was never actually Lincoln's bedroom. The room is decorated with furniture that is believed to have been owned by President Lincoln. Even though the bed is more than 8 feet (2.4 meters) long and 6 feet (1.8 meters) wide, large enough for such a tall man, he probably never even slept in it. Lincoln did use the room as an office and cabinet room. In this room on January 1, 1863, he signed the Emancipation Proclamation that ended slavery.

dining room. In 1877 Inauguration Day fell on a Sunday. Having a big public ceremony on a Sunday did not seem appropriate, so Rutherford B. Hayes took the oath of office in the Red Room. The next day a public ceremony was held at the Capitol.

The West Wing and the Oval Office

Today the president works in the Oval Office, which is located in the southeast corner of the West Wing. Here he meets with visiting leaders or works on speeches or policies with his staff. Presidents usually decorate the office with personal items such as photographs of family and friends. They may also make their own choice of antique desks and chairs from the White House storerooms to furnish the office. The furniture and decorations may vary from president to president, but two flags are always in place behind the president's chair. To his left is the Presidential Flag, and to his right is the flag of the United States.

In 1956 Vice President Richard Nixon posed in the Vice President's office, with the seal of office behind him. Nixon later became president.

Why oval?

The shape of the oval office was inspired by the oval Blue Room in the original building. George Washington preferred to host receptions in egg shaped rooms. Washington would stand by the fireplace as guests entered the room, bowed to him and took a place by the curved walls. When everyone had arrived, Washington would walk around the circle of guests and speak with each one. Some historians think Washington believed this arrangement was more democratic—everyone was an equal distance from the president.

The Cabinet Room is also located in the West Wing. This is a room in which the president meets with the heads of different departments. The room has an oval table surrounded by leather chairs. All of the chairs are the same height, except one. The President's chair is a little taller. The president often meets with the cabinet to discuss important issues of the day. President Warren G. Harding gave his dog, Laddie Boy, his own chair at cabinet meetings. There are other offices for staff and advisors in the West Wing, as well as a press briefing room. A free press that has access to the government is very important to the United States's **democracy**. Having the pressroom located in the same place as the president's office helps symbolize that importance.

The vice president's office

The vice president actually has two offices. One office is located in the West Wing, near the president. The other office is located in the Eisenhower Executive Office Building, located on the grounds of the White House. Today this office is used mainly for meetings and press interviews. Until 1974, vice presidents were responsible for finding their own place to live in Washington D.C. However, as housing prices got higher, Congress finally voted to repair a house owned by the Navy for the use of the vice president. The first vice president to live there was Walter Mondale in 1977.

Chapter Four:
Upstairs at the White House

With all the ceremony of **diplomatic** visits and state dinners, the hustle of tourists and cabinet meetings, the White House still serves as home to the president and his family. President William Henry Harrison lived there for only one month; Franklin Roosevelt lived there for twelve years. No matter how long or how short their stay, the president and his family have to adjust to the multipurpose White House.

The president and his family live on the second floor. The third floor contains the staff's living quarters and the guest rooms. Most presidential families have not lived in such a large home before moving to the White House. It has 132 rooms including 4 dining rooms, 3 elevators, 28 fireplaces, a bowling alley, a dentist office, a swimming pool, and a movie theater. Families try to make the White House feel like their own. They bring personal items to decorate their private rooms.

Many families feel overwhelmed by all the attention focused on them, but they try to live normal lives. They have friends over for dinner, watch television, or play cards. The children go to school, birthday parties, and sleepovers. But even while the family shares private time in their quarters at the White House, downstairs is busy with the activity of staff, guests, and tourists. President Reagan said that living at the White House was like living above a store.

First pets

Many presidents bring family pets to live with them at the White House. John Adams had a horse named Cleopatra. President Zachary Taylor's horse Old Whitney was allowed to graze on the lawn until it was discovered that tourists were plucking hairs from his tail for souvenirs. Macaroni and Leprechaun were Caroline and John Kennedy's ponies. Theodore Roosevelt's son Quentin gave his pony Algonquin a ride on the White House elevator.

President Bill Clinton's cat, Socks, gives a press conference.

Presidents have also been given animals as gifts. For a while, Jefferson had two grizzly bears that had been sent to him by the Lewis and Clark expedition. John Quincy Adams took care of the Marquis de Lafayette's alligator while the Frenchman toured the United States in 1824. The American **diplomat** in Siam, which is now Thailand, sent President Hayes the first Siamese cat to come to America. Another unusual present was a pair of tiny dogs that Commodore Perry brought back from Japan and gave to President Franklin Pierce.

Having fun

Recreation has always been an important part of family life at the White House. Jesse Grant, President Ulysses Grant's son, liked to look at the stars from the roof of the White House. Archie Roosevelt, President Theodore Roosevelt's son, coasted down the main staircase on a silver tray. His brother Quentin loved to walk on stilts in the Green Room, sometimes disturbing staff and tourists.

There are other ways to either relax or get exercise in the White House. President William J. Clinton jogged, and President George W. Bush rode a bike. President Franklin Roosevelt had polio and needed to swim to get exercise. A newspaper campaign raised enough money to build the White House pool. There is also an exercise gym, tennis court, a horseshoe court, and a putting green.

Preserving the People's House

In the 1800s and early 1900s, little was done to maintain the White House. In 1948 President Truman was alarmed to find out that the leg of his daughter's piano had broken through the upper level floor and knocked plaster down in the family dining room below. Engineers investigated and found that the house was almost ready to collapse. They said the walls were "standing up purely from habit." The exterior walls could be saved, but the interior had to be ripped out and replaced.

During construction, the Truman family moved across the street. A team of **architects** and contractors began supporting the original stone walls with concrete. Then they put up new steel framing at a cost of $6 million. The redone White House was finished in March 1952. President Truman celebrated by playing the East Room's great Steinway piano for viewers during a televised tour of the restored People's House.

Over the years, many of the original pieces of furniture and artwork had been sold or lost. Many valuable historic items had simply been stored away for decades and were never seen. In the 1960s, First Lady Jacqueline Kennedy wanted to make sure the White House and its treasures would be a protected legacy for future generations. Mrs. Kennedy's project established the idea of the White House as a living museum of American history. Later, President Johnson created the Committee for the Preservation of the White House to continue the work Mrs. Kennedy had started.

Today there is an office responsible for keeping track of the various items in the White House. The head of the office is known as the White House curator. A curator is the person responsible for collections in museums. Unlike most museums, the historic items in the White House—such as furniture, silverware, and china—are used everyday. Although they are used, all of these items are kept track of and repaired when necessary.

In addition to the items used daily, the White House also keeps many interesting items in storage. For example, when Jimmy Carter became president, his daughter Amy was a young girl. He designed and built a tree house for her in the yard. The designs and the actual tree house are now part of the White House collection.

Presidents come and go, but the White House remains the same. For over 200 years, it has remained the People's House, a treasured **symbol** of American **democracy**.

No matter who lives in the White House, it continues to belong to the American people.

Timeline

1790	Congress votes to establish a capitol city
1792	The cornerstone of the White House is laid in Washington, D.C.; the final design for President's House by James Hoban wins a design contest
1800	John and Abigail Adams move into unfinished White House
1801	First public reception held in the White House
1814	During the War of 1812, British soldiers capture Washington, D.C., and burn the White House
1817	James Monroe moves back into White House
1820s	South and North porticoes built, completing the White House as we know it today
1846	First photograph taken of the White House
1902	Renovation includes addition of the West Wing
1948	Discovery of cracking plaster leads to extensive renovation
2000	Four former presidents and five first ladies gather to celebrate the 200th anniversary of the White House

Further Information

Although touring the White House is free, you have to submit a request through your Member of Congress. To find out who your Member of Congress is, you can go online to www.house.gov.

Tours are available Tuesday through Saturday from 7:30 A.M. to 12:30 P.M.

You can also see a "virtual tour" of the White House online at www.whitehouse.gov. This site features fascinating information on the history of the White House and its residents.

If you are looking for information on a particular president, you may wish to visit his Presidential Library either in person or online. Information on these libraries can also be found at www.whitehouse.gov.

Further Reading

Giddens-White, Bryon. *The President and the Executive Branch.* Chicago: Heinemann, 2006.

Landau, Elaine. *The President's Work: The Executive Branch.* Minneapolis: Lerner Publications, 2003.

Sullivan, George E. Mr. President: *A Book of U.S. Presidents.* New York: Scholastic, 2001.

Glossary

ambassador official, or diplomat, who represents his government to another country

architect person who designs buildings and other large structures

capital town or city that is the official center or seat or government for the country

democracy government in which people represent themselves by voting

diplomat one who represents his or her country and meets regularly with people who represent foreign countries

executive branch one of the three branches of the U.S. government. The president is the head of the executive branch.

federal form of government consisting of separate states united under a central government

inauguration ceremony to swear a president into office

judicial branch one of the three branches of the U.S. government. The judicial branch is made up of the Supreme Court and other lower courts.

legislative branch one of the three branches of the U.S. government. The legislative branch is responsible for making laws.

patriotic showing a love for and pride in one's country

patriotism love for and pride in one's country

pavilion part of a building that sticks out from the rest, such as a porch

symbol something that stands for something else

veto overrule a proposed law

Index